THE *Declaration of Independence*

Our Government and Citizenship

SPIRIT
of America®

THE *Declaration of Independence*

By Kevin Cunningham

Content Adviser: Dr. Scott Douglas Gerber, Assistant Professor of Law, Law College, Ohio Northern University, Ada, Ohio

The Child's World
Chanhassen, Minnesota

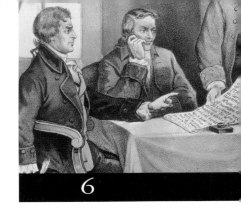

6

THE *Declaration of Independence*

Published in the United States of America by The Child's World®
PO Box 326 • Chanhassen, MN 55317-0326 • 800-599-READ • www.childsworld.com

Acknowledgments
The Child's World®: Mary Berendes, Publishing Director

Editorial Directions, Inc.: E. Russell Primm, Editorial Director; Pam Rosenberg, Line Editor; Katie Marsico, Associate Editor; Judi Shiffer, Associate Editor and Library Media Specialist; Matthew Messbarger, Editorial Assistant; Susan Hindman, Copy Editor; Lucia Raatma, Proofreader; Judith Frisbee, Peter Garnham, and Olivia Nellums, Fact Checkers; Tim Griffin/IndexServ, Indexer; Cian Loughlin O'Day, Photo Researcher; Linda S. Koutris, Photo Selector

Photo
Cover/frontispiece: Dick Frank/Corbis.
Interior: Corbis: 11 (Archivo Iconografico, S.A.), 15 (Bettmann), 23 (The Stapleton Collection), 28 (James P. Blair); Getty Images/Hulton|Archive: 9, 12, 16, 17; The Granger Collection: 6, 8, 10, 14, 19, 21, 25, 26.

Registration
The Child's World®, Spirit of America®, and their associated logos are the sole property and registered trademarks of The Child's World®.

Library of Congress Cataloging-in-Publication Data
Cunningham, Kevin (Kevin H.)
  The Declaration of Independence / by Kevin Cunningham.
    p. cm. — (Our government and citizenship)
  Includes index.
  ISBN 1-59296-325-0 (lib. bdg. : alk. paper) 1. United States. Declaration of Independence—Juvenile literature. 2. United States—Politics and government—1775–1783—Juvenile literature. I. Title. II. Series.
  E221.C86 2005
  973.3'13—dc22   2004006044

12　　　　　　　　21　　　　　　　　26

Contents

Chapter ONE

The Ideas behind the Declaration

IN JUNE 1776, THE **CONTINENTAL CONGRESS** AGREED that the 13 American colonies would separate from Great Britain. The Congress chose a group of five men—Thomas Jefferson, John Adams, Benjamin

The committee of five at work on the Declaration of Independence.

6

Franklin, Robert R. Livingston, and Roger Sherman—to write a document explaining the reasons behind this decision.

Jefferson, a Virginia farmer and the youngest of the group, was given the job of writing a draft, or first version, of the document. According to Adams, Jefferson had the "reputation of a masterly pen." Jefferson also came from the powerful colony of Virginia. Adams believed that "a Virginian ought to be at the head of this business," to convince the British and some doubtful Americans that the colonies stood together.

Jefferson wrote the draft of the Declaration of Independence in an apartment at Seventh and Market streets in Philadelphia. Much of the time, he sat at a special folding desk he had designed himself. He didn't know that the words flowing from his pen would become one of the most important documents in world history.

Many people think Thomas Jefferson came up with the ideas in the Declaration of Independence. Actually, Jefferson drew on ideas that were popular at the time. Some came from British law. After all, even if the colonists were getting ready to fight the British, they had been British subjects their entire lives. Other ideas were borrowed from thinkers in Scotland and France. Many of the thoughts expressed by Jefferson came from a new way of thinking called the Enlightenment.

The Enlightenment was not a single event. It was a change in attitudes, thinking, and beliefs that began in the late 1600s and continued through the 1700s. Before the Enlightenment, most people considered God responsible for every event, big or small. Bad weather and getting sick (or getting well) were among the many things considered "God's will."

During the 1600s, Newton and other scientists developed laws to explain things that were once considered God's will—not just weather and illness, but how to grow better crops and even why the planets moved through the sky. To them, all of nature, everything from flowers to the moons of Jupiter, operated on systems. Those systems obeyed laws of nature. By using science and reason, and by dismissing everything that could not be proven by facts, human beings could understand those laws. The Enlightenment, or Age of Reason, had begun.

Soon, thinkers applied the idea of systems and laws to every field of study, including politics and society. Because human beings existed as a part of nature, they must also be part of a system as well as part of the work of God. If you used reason to understand human nature, you could

Born in 1642, Sir Isaac Newton was an English physicist and mathematician.

understand why people did what they did and how each person fit into the system. If the system could be understood, society could be improved.

John Locke, an English philosopher, wrote several famous works on these topics. In one of his books, he wrote that the best government ruled "with the consent of the governed"—that is, with the permission of the people. Locke and others said that if human beings create a government, it must provide all citizens with the right to life, liberty, and property. That's the law of good government, a law of nature, which works the same for every human being.

The ideas of English philosopher John Locke had a great influence on the Founding Fathers of the United States.

A new religion also influenced Jefferson: Deism. According to Deism, God created the universe to operate like an enormous clock. The clock followed a set of laws. God started the clock and then let it run without interfering or, as Newton suggested, by only interfering to "reset" it from time to time. That idea was a big change from the days when people gave God credit or blame for everything.

Many of the **Founders** loved machines. They used images of machinery in their writing and tinkered with machinery in their everyday lives. Franklin was a professional printer. Jefferson's hero, David Rittenhouse, studied the stars, planets, and outer space. He built a famous orrery, a mechanical model of the solar system. James Small, one of Jefferson's teachers, built clocks.

Enlightenment thinkers assumed society could run like a machine, too. It just needed to be organized using the laws of nature put in motion by God. Such ideas from science, Locke, and the Enlightenment would form a major part of what Jefferson and the Founders had in mind for the new country.

David Rittenhouse was born in Germantown, Pennsylvania, in 1732.

10

JOHN LOCKE HAD TROUBLE DECIDING WHAT TO DO WITH HIS LIFE. HE WAS born in 1632 in the English village of Wrington and attended Oxford University. Eventually, he started a part-time medical practice.

By chance, he met the Earl of Shaftesbury, a man soon to become one of Britain's most powerful politicians. Not only did Locke help Shaftesbury with medical matters, he tutored the Earl's grandson. He also helped Shaftesbury with his government work. Eventually, Locke served in the government, too. But the cold, damp weather in London made him sick. In 1675, he began traveling around Europe, settling for a time in the sunny south of France. There he kept a journal and began to work out his soon-to-be-famous ideas concerning human nature and knowledge.

Locke went back to England in 1679. Unfortunately, Shaftesbury was involved in a series of problems with his enemies, including the king. Despite his money and power, he came close to facing charges of **treason.** Shaftesbury fled to the European continent in 1682 and soon died. Locke, under suspicion for helping his old friend, hid out in Holland.

When the trouble passed, Locke returned to government work to make money to pay his expenses while he wrote about philosophy. At age 57, he published *An Essay Concerning Human Understanding.* A later work, *Two Treatises of Government,* had a big influence on Jefferson and the other Founders.

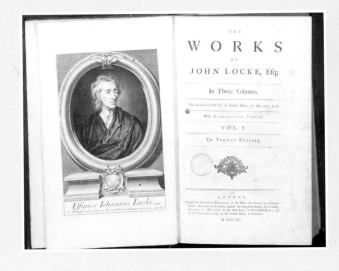

Though Locke was a late bloomer, his writings turned out to be very important to the Enlightenment, to Thomas Jefferson, and to the Declaration of Independence.

Chapter Two

Jefferson's World

American colonists fought with British soldiers at Lexington and Concord on April 19, 1775. These battles were the beginning of the American Revolution.

JEFFERSON'S WORK ON THE DECLARATION OF Independence came after more than a year of trouble and uncertainty in America. On April 19, 1775, colonists and British troops had clashed at Lexington, Massachusetts. Two months later, the

British won the Battle of Bunker Hill, but at the cost of 1,100 dead and wounded. In August, King George III, having refused to answer the colonies' complaints, declared his American subjects to be "in open and avowed **rebellion.**" Soon after, the British government passed a law stating that American ships and their goods could be seized.

The idea of independence began to take hold. Thomas Paine's pro-independence pamphlet *Common Sense* appeared in January 1776. In May, eight of the colonies agreed to support independence. Even those opposed to turning against Britain began to accept that revolution could not be avoided.

The Continental Congress took a break in June. Almost everyone expected the Congress to vote for independence when the representatives returned to Philadelphia. But the colonial leaders knew they needed a special document to explain the reasons behind the separation from Britain. For that purpose the Declaration of Independence listed the many grievances, or complaints, of the colonists.

At the same time, Americans knew they would not last long fighting Great Britain alone. They hoped for help from Britain's most powerful enemy—France. The French were already sending secret aid to the Americans. But France would openly assist the colonies only if they fought for

independence. If the Declaration of Independence even hinted that the Americans hoped to settle their differences with the British, France would ignore the document and the Americans' requests for help. Jefferson's language needed to leave no doubts.

It also had to convince the American colonists. Many colonists either did not wish to break from Britain or weren't sure. Some members of the Continental Congress and many ordinary colonists considered staying in the British Empire if the king would listen to their complaints. Ever since the clash at Lexington, colonists had argued for or against independence. Now those arguments became passionate. Were King George and his laws unfair? Families and towns split over the question.

Those in favor of a break from Britain—Adams, Franklin, Jefferson, George Washington, and others—knew they were suggesting a radical, or extreme, idea. Nearly everyone in the world answered to one kind of king or another. When Paine suggested that the American colonists were **unique** in their ability to choose their own leaders, the British called the idea ridiculous.

Colonists who supported the break wanted to turn their backs on Great Britain and the rest of Europe. In Europe, most people weren't truly free. It was impossible to get ahead unless you were born into the right family. Some colonists worried that if they did not break away, the same would happen to them. Rittenhouse spoke for many when he wished that "nature would raise her everlasting bars between the new and the old world; and make a voyage to Europe as impracticable as one to the moon."

What Rittenhouse and others had in mind was a society in which the government guaranteed each person's rights. Few believed

Thomas Paine's pamphlet, Common Sense, *helped convince many people that the colonies should fight for their independence from Great Britain.*

New York City as seen from the shores of New Jersey in the late 1700s.

every person was truly equal. They recognized some were smarter than others, some were stronger, some were more honest. But in the new America, each person would at least be treated the same under the law and have a chance to succeed.

Thomas Jefferson and the committee assigned to write the Declaration of Independence had to keep all of this, and more, in mind as they worked.

16

GEORGE III IS OFTEN REMEMBERED AS A **TYRANT** WHO TAXED TEA, MADE UNFAIR laws, and forced colonists to house British soldiers. From the king's point of view, though, the American colonies cost a lot of money to develop and guard. Why shouldn't the colonists pay their fair share of the expenses?

These days, historians don't consider George evil. Even during the early days of the country, many Americans recognized that some of the charges against the king stretched the truth. Strong language was needed to inspire **patriots,** but it was not always accurate.

However, George definitely had flaws as a leader. Too often he appointed weak advisers to boss around, instead of talented men who could help him lead. When the Americans complained about unfair laws, he turned a deaf ear. Worse, he refused to quit fighting when it became obvious Britain couldn't win the war.

In his defense, George suffered from a serious illness. It may have influenced some of his bad decisions. Many historians believe the illness was porphyria, which can cause symptoms such as confusion, anxiousness, and depression. That may explain the tales of "Mad King George."

In 1788, the king became so sick that plans were made to replace him. He got better for a while, but by 1811 his son, George IV, had to take over. George III spent the last years of his life at Windsor Castle, blind and insane. He died in 1820.

Chapter THREE

The Declaration

AFTER THOMAS JEFFERSON FINISHED HIS DRAFT of the Declaration of Independence, the other members of the committee—Adams, Franklin, Livingston, and Sherman—made minor changes. The edited version then went to the Continental Congress for review. The members of Congress made more changes—including some that addressed the issue of slavery—and rewrote the conclusion.

The Declaration of Independence begins with an explanation of why the document has been written:

> When in the Course of human events, it becomes necessary for one people to dissolve the political bands which have connected them with another, and to assume among the powers of the earth, the separate and equal station to which the Laws of Nature and of Nature's God entitle them, a decent respect to the opinions of mankind requires

---

Interesting Fact

▶ Jefferson did not appreciate that Adams, Franklin, and other representatives of Congress changed his original draft. Later on, he made copies of the original to show others how they had **"mutilated"** his work.

that they should declare the causes which impel them to the separation.

In this introduction, the authors use the popular Enlightenment idea that all things in the world obey the laws of nature. They state that they are entitled to form a separate and equal country under the laws of nature and announce that they will give their reasons for breaking away from Great Britain.

The next sentence is one of the most famous sentences in American history:

We hold these truths to be self-evident, that all men are created equal, that they are

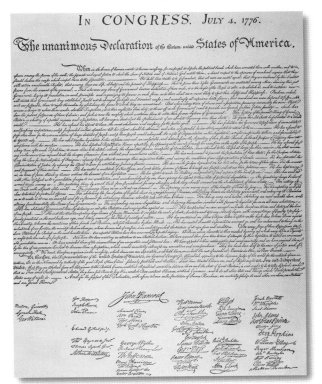

The original Declaration of Independence has been kept at the National Archives building in Washington, D.C., since 1952.

George III's 60-year reign (1760–1820) is one of the longest in British history, second only to Queen Victoria's 63 years (1837–1901).

endowed by their Creator with certain unalienable Rights, that among these are Life, Liberty and the pursuit of Happiness.

Enlightenment thinkers, including Locke, liked to declare their ideas "self-evident." A self-evident idea is one that is so obvious that any intelligent person must agree with it. By starting this way, Jefferson and the Founders were saying that it was impossible to argue with their statements. All men are created equal. Period. Not just Americans. *All* men. Like gravity and all laws of nature, these rights apply to everyone and cannot be changed.

The next sentence states that government gains its powers from "the consent of the governed." When the government acts against the people, the people have a right to "alter or to abolish it, and to institute new Government." Here, the writers make the argument that the king has not protected the rights of the people. As a result, the people can get rid of him and create a new government that respects their rights.

In several places Jefferson used strong words, such as *tyranny.* Not everyone agreed this should be done. John Adams, for one, thought calling King George a tyrant was "too much like scolding." He thought the document should remain cool and reasoned.

The Declaration of Independence goes on to list the colonist's grievances against King George. All of them prevented, in one way or another, "life, liberty, and the pursuit of happiness."

The authors first lay out how the king has mistreated the colonists. Without a doubt, most of the grievances were true. He made it difficult for the lawmakers in each colony to pass the laws they needed to govern their colonies. He taxed the colonists without allowing them to vote for or against the taxes. He kept troops in the colonies against American wishes, including (at times) in people's houses. More than once he broke up elected bodies of representatives when they disagreed with him.

The authors then charge that George is trying to destroy the colonies. Among other things, he is waging war, burning towns, killing people, and hiring soldiers and Indians to attack colonists.

In response to all these wrongs, the authors go on to say, the American colonists have tried to be reasonable:

> In every stage of these Oppressions We have Petitioned for Redress in the most humble terms: Our repeated Petitions have been answered only by repeated injury.

They say that the colonists have complained politely, and in return King George has continued

British troops were stationed in Boston to calm colonial unrest over the passage of the Stamp Act.

▶ On the night of July 4, 1776, Philadelphia printer John Dunlap made an unknown number of copies of the Declaration of Independence. Today, 24 copies of these "Dunlap broadsides" still exist.

to hurt them. Because the king insists on acting like a tyrant, he is "unfit to be the ruler of a free people." The authors go on to remind readers that the colonists tried to get the help of the British people and they, too, ignored the complaints.

Finally, having concluded that the colonists have no choice but to break away from Great Britain, the authors declare the colonies to be "free and independent states." The new United States of America no longer owes loyalty to King George, is no longer connected to Great Britain, and can act like any independent country.

The Declaration concludes with another famous phrase:

> And for the support of this Declaration, with a firm reliance on the protection of divine Providence, we mutually pledge to each other our Lives, our Fortunes and our sacred Honor.

The Founders saw a tough war ahead. Here they vowed to do whatever was necessary to see it through. Later, two of the document's signers put the paragraph in plainer language. "There must be no pulling different ways," said John Hancock, president of the Continental Congress. "We must all hang together."

"Yes," Ben Franklin said. "We must all hang together, or most assuredly we shall all hang separately."

THERE ARE MANY MYTHS ABOUT THE DECLARATION OF INDEPENDENCE. THE biggest is that the members of the Continental Congress gathered on July 4, 1776, and signed their names to the document. Not only did it not happen on July 4, but in a few cases, the signings didn't even take place in 1776.

Congress met on July 1, 1776. The next day they adopted a resolution for independence. The representatives then began to debate the Declaration, finally agreeing to its words on July 4. Only one man signed the document that day: John Hancock, the president of the Congress. His signature was witnessed by Charles Thompson, the secretary.

Not every state voted to approve the document on July 4. New York's representatives had to wait for permission. They finally cast their votes on July 9. Ten days later, on the 19th, Congress agreed to prepare the Declaration of Independence as an official government document. The representatives met on August 2 to sign their names to this document. They went geographically by state, from north to south—New Hampshire first and Georgia last.

A few members of the Congress chose not to sign. Robert Livingston, a member of the committee that drafted the Declaration, thought it was too soon for independence. A handful of the signers happened to be away on August 2. They added their signatures later. In the case of Delaware's Thomas McKean (right), it was much later. He left Philadelphia in early July to join Washington's army. It took until 1781 for him to add his name.

The Declaration in Action

IN 1776 THE FOUNDERS NEEDED THE DECLARATION to explain why America must separate from Great Britain. In the 1800s, people read the document differently. The "self-evident" truth that "all men are created equal" became the foundation for new ideas about what the United States stood for and what its citizens believed in. Those ideas met a challenge right away: slavery.

From the beginning, the Founders saw a huge contrast between slavery and the words about freedom in the Declaration. In his original draft, Jefferson blamed the slave trade on King George. Adams considered this paragraph one of the best parts of the Declaration. But such words could never stay in. Congress wanted the document to draw the colonies together. Nearly half of the men who signed the Declaration of Independence owned slaves. Many became rich because of the slave trade. Leaving in an antislavery paragraph would divide the colonies—and only together could they defeat Great Britain. After a heated debate, Congress cut out the paragraph.

In the mid-1800s, the slavery fight turned bitter. By then, only the southern states supported slavery. **Abolitionists** often quoted the statement from the Declaration of Independence that "all men are created equal" and argued that this was a God-given law of nature. According to southern politician John C. Calhoun, though, the Declaration was wrong:

> [Liberty] is a reward to be earned, not a blessing to be gratuitously lavished on all alike; a reward reserved for the intelligent, the patriotic, the virtuous and deserving.

Even many opposed to slavery agreed with part of Calhoun's statement. Taking the Declaration *too* seriously meant giving equal rights not just to African-Americans but to groups such as Native Americans, women, and foreigners. To many Americans in the 1800s, that was going too far. Yet in his Gettysburg Address, Lincoln used the phrase "all men are created equal" to introduce his ideas and to hint that the Civil War was being fought to defend that thought:

Interesting Fact

▶ On July 2, 1777, Vermont became the first state to outlaw slavery.

John C. Calhoun served the United States as a congress-man, senator, secretary of war, secretary of state, and seventh vice-president. He was strongly in favor of states' rights and spoke out in defense of slavery.

Fourscore and seven years ago our Fathers brought forth upon this continent a new nation, conceived in Liberty, and dedicated to the proposition that all men are created equal.

The Declaration of Independence, far from being forgotten or dismissed, grew in importance. South American rebels fighting against Spain and Portugal were inspired by it. In the United States, the constitutions of many states began with some version of "all men are created equal." Workers and farmers used its words and ideas to demand equality.

Susan B. Anthony and Elizabeth Cady Stanton speak at a meeting of the National Woman's Suffrage Association in the 1870s.

One group even dared to say, "We hold these truths to be self-evident: that all men and women are created equal." On July 19–20, 1848, about 300 people—two-thirds of them women—met in Seneca Falls, New York. Led by Elizabeth Cady Stanton and the abolitionist Lucretia Mott, the participants drew up a document based on the Declaration of Independence. In its list of grievances, this new document argued that women had the right to vote, to go to college, and to work in professions such as law and medicine. It also said that they should not be treated as the property of their husbands. It was the first women's rights meeting in U.S. history.

In 1948, the United Nations borrowed the Declaration's ideas for the Universal Declaration of Human Rights: "All human beings are born free and equal in dignity and rights. They are endowed with reason and conscience. . . ."

Not surprisingly, African-Americans fighting for equal rights often quoted the Declaration of Independence. Martin Luther King Jr. spoke of the Declaration of Independence in his famous "I have a dream" speech, delivered in 1963.

> When the architects of our republic wrote the magnificent words of the Constitution and the Declaration of Independence, they were signing a promissory note to which every American was to fall heir.
>
> This note was a promise that all men would be guaranteed the inalienable rights of life, liberty, and the pursuit of happiness.

The National Committee of Black Churchmen, in 1970, quoted the document's self-evident truth of equality. The group added that when others refuse to treat them equally, "Men are bound by self-

▶ Today's Republican Party was born in March 1854 in Ripon, Wisconsin. It was made up of people opposed to slavery and people who wanted to settle western lands. They chose the name *Republican* in memory of Thomas Jefferson's Democratic-Republican Party.

▶ A marble bust of John Adams was one of the first to be made for the vice-presidential bust collection that was authorized by the Senate in 1886. The sculpture was done by Daniel Chester French in 1889. French also sculpted the statue of Abraham Lincoln that sits in the Lincoln Memorial in Washington, DC.

respect and honor to rise up in righteous indignation." Jefferson had also mentioned honor at the end of the Declaration.

Today, the Declaration of Independence continues to serve as a model for world leaders. Its ideas still influence those writing documents that outline systems of government for countries around the world.

The Declaration of Independence is far more than an ancient document kept under glass. Its authors meant it to be a bold statement of what the United States stands for—or should stand for—and what all countries should strive to achieve. The document's words challenge us to live up to its lofty goals. Because it set such high goals, the Declaration of Independence remains vital—not just for what it inspired yesterday, but for what it gives us today and where it might lead us tomorrow.

The Thomas Jefferson Memorial in Washington, D.C., was dedicated on April 13, 1943, the 200th anniversary of Jefferson's birth.

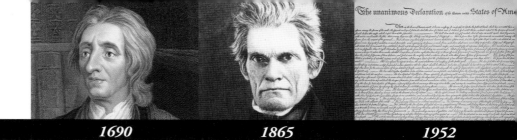
1690 John Locke publishes his *Two Treatises on Government.*

1775 On April 19, British soldiers clash with American militiamen near Lexington, Massachusetts.

1776 Thomas Jefferson and others are appointed on June 11 to draft a declaration of independence; Congress approves an edited version on July 4; most of the signers sign their names to the Declaration of Independence on August 2.

1781 Surrounded by American and French forces, Britain's General Cornwallis surrenders at Yorktown on October 19.

1783 The Treaty of Paris officially ends the American Revolution.

1826 Thomas Jefferson and John Adams both die on July 4, the 50th anniversary of the approval of the Declaration of Independence.

1841 The parchment copy of the Declaration of Independence is hung on a wall at what is now the National Portrait Gallery in Washington, D.C.; over the next 35 years, it is damaged by exposure to direct sunlight.

1848 Elizabeth Cady Stanton and Lucretia Mott organize the Seneca Falls Convention, the first women's rights meeting in U.S. history.

1865 The Thirteenth Amendment officially ends slavery.

1903 The Declaration of Independence is placed in a steel safe to save it from further damage.

1941 In December, the government moves the Declaration to Fort Knox, Kentucky, for safekeeping after the December 7 attack on Pearl Harbor.

1944 The Declaration is returned to Washington, D.C., in October.

1948 The United Nations adopts the Universal Declaration of Human Rights.

1952 The Declaration of Independence is moved to the National Archives Building, its current home.

1963 Martin Luther King Jr. speaks about the Declaration of Independence in his "I have a dream" speech.

1970 The National Committee of Black Churchmen issues a call for equal rights that contains language based on the Declaration of Independence.

abolitionists (ab-uh-LISH-uh-nists)
Abolitionists are people who fought to end slavery, especially before the Civil War. Many abolitionists attended the Seneca Falls Convention to support equal rights for women.

Continental Congress (KON-tuh-nehn-tuhl KONG-gris)
The Continental Congress was the group of representatives from each of the original 13 American colonies who met to make decisions on matters that affected all of the colonies during the time of the American Revolution. The Continental Congress agreed that the 13 colonies would declare their independence from Great Britain.

Founders (FOUN-durs)
Founders are the people who establish something, such as an organization or a country. The leaders who established the United States of America as a country separate from Great Britain are often called the Founders, or Founding Fathers, of the United States.

mutilated (MYOO-tuh-lay-ted)
If something is mutilated it is seriously injured or damaged. Thomas Jefferson believed that his original draft of the Declaration of Independence was mutilated by those who revised it.

patriots (PAY-tree-uhts)
Patriots are people who love their country and will support it, even if means fighting in a war. The Declaration of Independence used strong language to inspire American patriots.

rebellion (rih-BELL-yun)
A rebellion is an uprising against authority. When the colonists refused to obey Britain's government, the king declared them to have started a rebellion.

treason (TREE-zun)
Treason is the crime of trying to overthrow a leader or government by helping out an enemy. John Locke almost faced charges of treason for his friendship with the Earl of Shaftesbury.

tyrant (TIE-ruhnt)
A tyrant is a cruel and brutal leader. Thomas Jefferson accused King George of being a tyrant for his unfair treatment of the colonists.

unique (yoo-NEEK)
Something that is unique is the only one of its kind. Thomas Paine suggested that the American colonists were unique in their ability to choose their own leaders.

For Further INFORMATION

At the Library

Fink, Sam. *The Declaration of Independence.* New York: Scholastic Reference, 2002.

Freedman, Russell. *Give Me Liberty!: The Story of the Declaration of Independence.* New York: Holiday House, 2000.

Harness, Cheryl. *Thomas Jefferson.* Washington, D.C.: National Geographic, 2004.

On the Web

Visit our home page for lots of links about the Declaration of Independence:
http://www.childsworld.com/links.html

Note to Parents, Teachers, and Librarians:
We routinely verify our Web links to make sure they're safe, active sites—so encourage your readers to check them out!

Places to Visit or Contact

Independence National Historical Park
To visit Independence Hall and learn more about the Declaration of Independence and the Founders of the United States
143 South Third Street
Philadelphia, PA 19106
215/597-8974

The National Archives Building
To see the Declaration of Independence, the Constitution, and the Bill of Rights and learn more about these important documents
700 Pennsylvania Avenue NW
Washington, DC 20408
866/272-6272

Index

About the Author

KEVIN CUNNINGHAM IS AN AUTHOR AND TRAVEL WRITER. HE studied journalism and history at the University of Illinois at Urbana. His other books include *Condoleezza Rice: Educator and Presidential Adviser, Power to the People: How We Elect the President and Other Officials,* and *The Declaration of Independence.* He lives in Chicago.